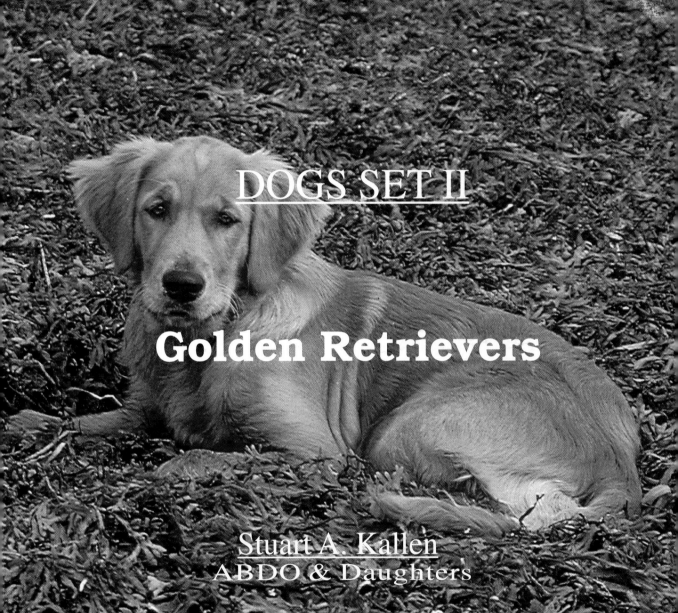

DOGS SET II

Golden Retrievers

Stuart A. Kallen
ABDO & Daughters

visit us at
www.abdopub.com

Published by Abdo & Daughters, 4940 Viking Drive, Suite 622, Edina, Minnesota 55435.

Printed in the United States.

Cover Photo credits: Peter Arnold, Inc.
Interior Photo credits: Peter Arnold, Inc.

Edited by Bob Italia

Library of Congress Cataloging-in-Publication Data

Kallen, Stuart., 1955-
  Golden retrievers / Stuart Kallen.
    p. cm. -- (Dogs. Set II)
  Includes index.
  Summary: An introduction to this friendly dog, which includes its history, development, uses, and care.
  ISBN 1-56239-576-9
  1. Golden retrievers--Juvenile literature. [1. Golden retrievers. 2. Dogs.] I. Title. II. Series: Kallen, Stuart A., 1955- Dogs. Set II.
  SF429.G63K35 1998
  636.752'7--dc21   97-15716
                                                         CIP
                                                         AC
Revised Edition 2002

Contents

Dogs and Wolves— Close Cousins

Dogs have been living with humans for more than 12,000 years. Today, millions of dogs live in the world. Over 400 **breeds** exist. And, believe it or not, all dogs are related to the wolf.

Some dogs—like tiny poodles or Great Danes— may look nothing like wolves. But under their skin, dogs share many feelings and **traits** with wolves.

The dog family is called Canidae, from the Latin word *canis*, meaning "dog." The canid family has 37 **species**. They include foxes, jackals, wild dogs, and wolves.

Opposite page: Dogs and wolves share some of the same traits.

Golden Retrievers

In the early 1800s, hunting was an important way for people to get food. In England and Scotland hunting was also a sport. Retriever-type dogs were very popular. They would pick up ducks and other game and return it to the hunters. The golden retriever was bred by Sir Dudley Marjoriebanks when he crossed bloodhounds, setters, and retrievers. Today the golden retriever is one of the most popular dogs in the United States.

Golden retrievers are bred to find ducks in water. They have soft mouths so they don't chew up the birds. They have thick **coats** that protect them in the coldest water.

Opposite page: A golden retriever bringing back a duck.

What They're Like

Golden retrievers are strong and smart. They can run all day, retrieve game, and sit by your feet all night. Golden retrievers are easy to train. They are eager learners, very loyal, and very patient. These dogs are friendly and gentle. They are even-tempered and get along well with children and families.

Golden retrievers have been trained as **Seeing Eye dogs**. They love to play fetch with a ball or frisbee. They are also good hunting dogs and show dogs. Because of their intelligence, beauty, loyalty, and steady nerves, golden retrievers make a perfect family pet.

Opposite page: A golden retriever catching a frisbee.

Coat and Color

Golden retrievers have thick **coats** that are dense and water repellent. They have good undercoats that protect them from cold water. The fur is softer than a short-haired dog and more coarse than a long-haired dog. The hair lays flat on the body and may be straight or wavy. The fur is "feathered" on the back of their legs.

A golden retriever has a rich golden color. It should not have any white or black hair. Its eyes are friendly and show intelligence. The dark brown eyes should never be lighter than the coat. The nose is black or dark brown.

Opposite page: Golden retrievers are a rich golden color.

Size

Male golden retrievers are about 24 inches (60 cm) from the ground to their shoulders. Females are slightly smaller. Male dogs should weigh between 65 and 75 pounds (29 to 34 kg), and females from 55 to 65 pounds (25 to 29 kg).

The golden retriever has a broad head with a wide face. The ears are medium short, hanging flat against the head. They have rounded tips that end slightly below the jaw. The neck is medium long, sloping well back into the shoulders. The body is well balanced and muscular. The feet are medium sized, round, and compact with thick pads. The tail is carried with an upward curve and is feathered with thick hair.

The golden retriever has a broad head with a wide face.

Care

Golden retrievers make happy members of any family. They are people-pleasers.

Like any dog, a golden retriever needs the same things a human needs: a warm bed, food, water, exercise, and lots of love.

Golden retrievers have long hair that needs to be brushed once a week. Sometimes the dog will need a bath and its nails clipped. All dogs need shots every year. These shots stop diseases such as **distemper** and **hepatitis**.

As a member of your household, your dog expects love and attention. Golden retrievers enjoy human contact and like to play fetch. They love to run and explore.

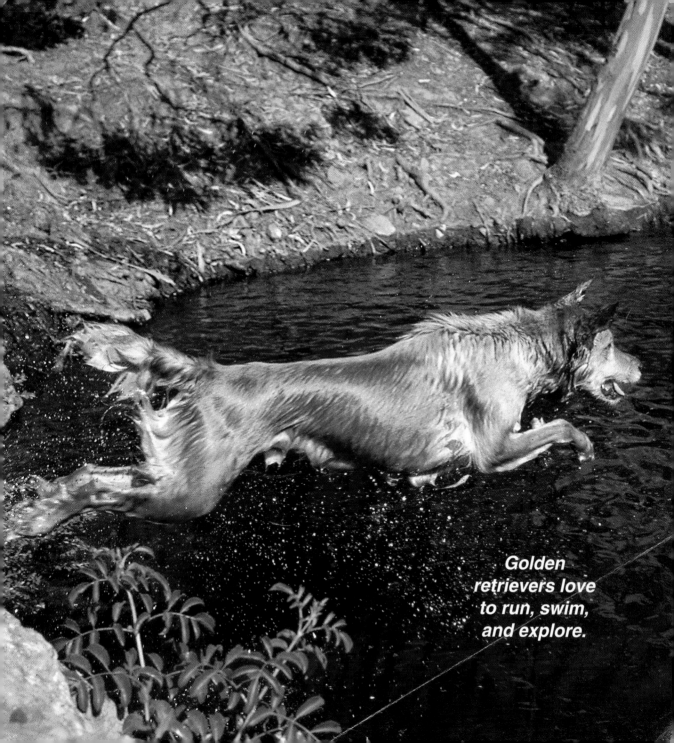

Golden retrievers love to run, swim, and explore.

Feeding

Like all dogs, golden retrievers eat meat. But they need a well-balanced diet. Most dog foods—dry or canned—will give the dog proper **nutrition**.

If you buy a puppy, find out what it has been eating and continue the diet. A small puppy needs four or five small meals a day. By six months, it will need only two meals a day. By one year, a single evening feeding will be enough.

Golden retrievers must be exercised every day so they do not gain weight. Walking, running, and playing together will keep you and your dog happy and healthy. Give your dog a hard rubber ball to play with.

Like any animal, these dogs need fresh water. Keep water next to the dog's food bowl and change it daily.

Like any dog, a golden retriever needs a well-balanced diet.

Things They Need

Dogs need quiet places to sleep. A soft dog bed in a quiet corner is the best place for a golden retriever to sleep. Golden retrievers should live indoors. If the dog must live outside, give it a dry, **insulated** dog house.

Golden retrievers love to play and explore. A fenced-in yard is the perfect home for this kind of dog. If that is not possible, use a chain on a runner.

In most cities and towns, a dog must be leashed when going for a walk. It also needs a license. A dog license has the owner's name, address, and telephone number on it. If the dog runs away, the owner can be called.

Opposite page: Golden retrievers like a soft bed in a quiet corner to sleep.

Puppies

A golden retriever can have up to eight puppies. The dog is **pregnant** for about nine weeks. When she is ready to give birth, she prefers a dark place away from noises. If your dog is pregnant, give her a strong box lined with an old blanket. She will have her puppies there.

Puppies are tiny and helpless when born. They arrive about a half hour apart. The mother licks them to get rid of the birth sacs and to help them start breathing. Their eyes are shut, making them blind for their first nine days. They are also deaf for about ten days.

Dogs are **mammals**. This means they drink milk from their mother. After about four weeks, puppies begin to grow teeth. Separate them from their mother and give the puppies soft dog food.

A golden retriever puppy.

Glossary

breed: a grouping of animals with the same traits.

coat: the dog's outer covering of hair.

distemper: a contagious disease caused by a virus that dogs and other animals can get.

hepatitis (hep-uh-TIE-tis): an inflammation of the liver caused by virus.

insulation (in-suh-LAY-shun): something that stops heat loss.

mammal: a group of animals, including humans, that have hair and feed their young milk.

nutrition (new-TRISH-un): food; nourishment.

pregnant: with one or more babies growing inside the body.

Seeing Eye dog: a dog that is trained to help a person who is blind.

species (SPEE-sees): a kind or type.

trait: a feature of an animal.

veterinarian: a doctor trained to take care of animals.

Internet Sites

AKC Standard for Golden Retrievers
http://www.american-research.com/draper-kennel/akc.html
The information contained in this web-site is designed to inform individuals who are interested in obtaining a Golden Retriever. It explains the basic qualities and characteristics which Goldens possess.

Shamvali Golden Retrievers
http://www.ohio.net/~paulquay/
Shamvali welcomes you. If you are interested in quality golden puppies this is the home page for you! Twenty-four years breeding quality golden retrievers. This home page helps find Golden puppies.

The American Kennel Club Online
http://www.akc.org/
The American Kennel Club can help you begin your research with its pictures and descriptions of each breed recognized by the AKC. Your initial research will help you narrow the field when it comes to selecting the breed for you and your lifestyle. Remember to consider your dog's lifestyle, too. And for extended research, consult the resources at your local library.

These sites are subject to change. Go to your favorite search engine and type in Golden Retrievers for more sites.

Index